A Visit to
ISRAEL

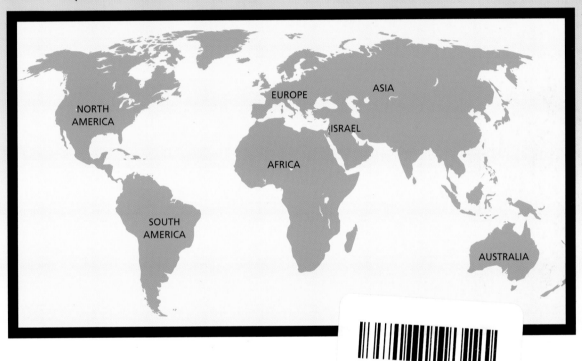

NORTH AMERICA

SOUTH AMERICA

EUROPE

ASIA

ISRAEL

AFRICA

AUSTRALIA

D1289072

Peter & Connie Roop

Heinemann LIBRARY

LONDON PUBLIC LIBRARY

First published in Great Britain by Heinemann Library
Halley Court, Jordan Hill, Oxford OX2 8EJ
a division of Reed Educational and Professional Publishing Ltd.
Heinemann is a registered trademark of Reed Educational & Professional Publishing Limited.

OXFORD MELBOURNE AUCKLAND KUALA LUMPUR
SINGAPORE IBADAN NAIROBI KAMPALA JOHANNESBURG
GABORONE PORTSMOUTH NH CHICAGO

Designed by AMR
Illustrations by Art Construction
Printed in Hong Kong / China

02 01 00 99
10 9 8 7 6 5 4 3 2 1

ISBN 0 431 08322 3
This title is also available in a hardback library edition (ISBN 0 431 08313 4).

British Library Cataloguing in Publication Data

Roop, Peter
  A visit to Israel
  1. Israel – Social conditions – Juvenile literature
  2. Israel – Geography – Juvenile literature
  3. Israel – Social life and customs – Juvenile literature
  I.Title II.Israel
  956.9·4·054

Acknowledgements
The Publishers would like to thank the following for permission to reproduce photographs:
J Allan Cash Ltd: pp7, 10, 11, 12, 16, 17, 20; Hutchison Library: p13, R Francis p25, M Friend p14,
J Henderson p18; Images Colour Library: pp8, 9; Israel Tourist Office: p29; Magnum: Abbas pp21, 24,
F Mayer p22, D Stock p19; Panos Pictures: H Davies pp15, 23, G Mansfield p6; Performing Arts Library:
C Barda p28; Trip: H Rogers p27, S Shapiro p26, A Tovy p5

Cover photograph reproduced with permission of Carlos Reyes-Manzo Andes Press Agency

Every effort has been made to contact copyright holders of any material reproduced in this
book. Any omissions will be rectified in subsequent printings if notice is given to the Publisher.

Any words appearing in bold, **like this**, are explained in the Glossary.

Contents

Israel

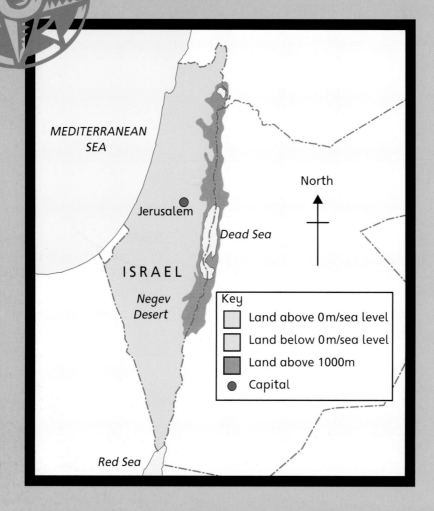

MEDITERRANEAN
SEA

North

Jerusalem

Dead Sea

ISRAEL

Negev
Desert

Key
- Land above 0m/sea level
- Land below 0m/sea level
- Land above 1000m
- Capital

Red Sea

Israel is one of the smallest countries
in the world. It lies on a thin strip of
land between the Mediterranean
Sea and four other countries.

The modern country of Israel was formed
50 years ago in 1948. Although **Arab**
people lived there, it was given to the
Jews. They came from all around the
world to live there.

Land

Israel has mountains, **valleys** and **deserts**. Half of the country is a desert called the Negev.

Israel has hot, dry summers. Winters are cool and wet. This is good weather for farmers to grow large **crops** of fruit and vegetables.

Landmarks

The Dead Sea is so salty that fish and plants cannot live in it. All the salt in the water stops people from sinking. They just float on top!

Jerusalem is Israel's **capital** and its largest and oldest city. People have lived there for 5000 years. It is a holy city for **Jews, Christians** and **Muslims**.

Homes

In the cities, most people live in small houses or flats. There is not much space for them to have gardens.

In the country, people live on their own farms or kibbutzim. Kibbutzim are where many families live and work together as one large family.

Food

Much of the food in Israel is kosher.
Kosher means that food is prepared and
served following special Jewish rules.
Lunch is the main meal of the day.

Fruit and vegetables are eaten with
every meal. Felafel is a favourite dish.
It is a fried food made from chick peas.

Clothes

Most Israelis wear clothes like yours.
In the hot weather they wear cotton
clothes which are cooler.

Some **Jews** wear black hats and clothes as part of their **religion**. **Arabs** often wear robes and **headdresses**.

Work

Farmers have learned how to grow **crops** in the **desert**. They are very careful not to waste water. They grow cotton, wheat, fruit, vegetables and olives.

Most of Israel's factories are in the cities.
They make machines, weapons, radios,
televisions, computers and cloth.

Transport

Israel is so small that it does not take long to travel from one end to the other by bus or car. There are aeroplanes and trains, too.

Bedouins in the Negev **Desert** use
donkeys to carry their loads. Bedouins
move their tents from place to place
to find water for their animals.

19

Language

Four out of five people in Israel are Jewish. They speak and write Hebrew, the **ancient** Jewish language. Signposts are written in Hebrew, Arabic and English.

Most of the non-**Jews** in Israel are **Arabs**.
They speak and write Arabic. This language
has 28 letters and like Hebrew it is read
from right to left.

School

Jewish children go to school every day except Saturday. Saturday is their day off to rest, play and pray. At school they study Hebrew, Arabic, maths, science, history and English.

Arab children have their own schools.
Their day off is Sunday. They study maths,
science, history, Arabic and English.

Free time

Football (soccer) is the most popular Israeli sport. Many people enjoy basketball and tennis, too.

Many Israelis enjoy long walks in the
countryside or helping on farms or
kibbutzim. At the Red Sea they
enjoy water sports like **snorkelling**,
swimming and wind surfing.

Celebrations

Rosh Hashanah is the Jewish New Year. It is celebrated in September for two days. Children and their families enjoy special foods like apples and honey.

Hanukkah is the Jewish festival of lights. It takes place in winter for eight nights. People light special candles. There is a candle for every night of the festival.

The Arts

Going to a play or concert is popular in Israel. Many famous musicians, like Zubin Mehta, have come from Israel.

Singing and dancing are very popular, too. Many Israelis dance the **hora** in parks on Saturday evenings. Films are a favourite indoor entertainment.

29

Factfile

Name   The full name of Israel is the State of Israel.

Capital   The **capital** city of Israel is Jerusalem.

Languages   Most Israelis speak Hebrew, Arabic or English.

Population There are more than 5 million people living in Israel.

Money   Instead of the dollar or pound, the Israelis have the shekel.

Religions   Most Israelis believe in Judaism or **Islam**.

Products   Israel produces lots of machinery, diamonds, chemicals, cloth, fruit and vegetables.

Words you can learn

ehhad (eh-KHAD)	one
shtayim	two
shalosh (sha-LOSH)	three
shalom (sha-LOM)	hello
shalom	goodbye
todah (to-DAH)	thank you
bevkasha (be-va-ka-SHA)	please
ken	yes
loh	no

Glossary

ancient	from a long time ago
Arab	the people living in north Africa or western parts of Asia (called the Middle East) – many of them are Muslims
Bedouin	a group of people who live in tents in the desert
capital	the city where the government is based
Christians	the people who believe in Jesus Christ
crops	the plants that farmers grow
deserts	large areas of land that have little or no rain and very few plants or animals
headdresses	pieces of cloth tied around the head
hora	a well-known Jewish dance that can be danced in a circle
Islam	the religion of the Arabs
Jews	the people who believe in the Judaic religion
Muslims	the people who believe in the Islamic religion
orchestra	a large group of musicians
religion	what people believe in
snorkelling	swimming under water with breathing equipment
temple	a usually very grand building used as a place of worship
valleys	the low areas between the higher hill tops or mountains

Index